MAKING THINGS SPECIAL

Tech Design Leadership from the Trenches

by Hillel Cooperman & Jenny Lam

Edited by Scott Berkun
Illustrated by Tom Chang

JACKSON FISH MARKET PUBLISHING

Jackson Fish Market Publishing

1425 Broadway #448

Seattle, WA 98122

www.jacksonfish.com

Ordering Information: Quantity sales. Special discounts are available on quantity purchases by corporations, associations, and others. For details, contact Jackson Fish Market Publishing at (206) 724-4144 or visit www.makingthingsspecial.com.

Printed in the United States of America

Publisher's Cataloging-in-Publication data
Cooperman, Hillel; Lam, Jenny.
Making Things Special : Tech Design Leadership from the Trenches / Hillel Cooperman and Jenny Lam.
Typeset in Minion Pro – an Adobe Original typeface by Robert Slimbach, Whitney by Hoefler & Co., and Helsing by Great Lakes Lettering.
p. cm.
ISBN 978-1936093694
1. The main category of the book —Design —Business. 2. Art

First Edition

14 13 12 11 10 / 10 9 8 7 6 5 4 3 2 1

CONTENTS

Making Things Special

PREFACE

Hi. Welcome to our book. :)

If you're reading this, it's probably because you love beautifully crafted, eminently enjoyable technology experiences and would like to help create one yourself. You're probably a designer or someone who appreciates great design but hasn't had the formal training. And yet, the job of creating these technology experiences is not a solo effort. It takes a team. And most teams dedicated to the creation of technology are not led by designers. This is not in dispute.

But disputes are likely in your future.

No matter how good a designer you are, no matter how educated, experienced, thoughtful, and talented, there will be people who are not designers, or even design-savvy, who will likely get in your way. They may do this inadvertently. They may do this out of ignorance.

And in some cases, they may do it out of willfulness. But this is inevitable.

This book is for you.

If you're a designer in a non-design led organization, it will help you move the organization, and the product you care about, in the right direction.

If you're not a designer but want to move your non-design led organization in the right direction, this book will help you do that.

Ultimately, there's no magic bullet to change our industry to make design its top priority. This is a battle that will be fought in the trenches – by you. But every product you put out, every experience you create, that is better designed, more customer-centric, and even more thoughtful, will raise the bar further, and create incentives for the rest of the industry to follow suit.

So good luck, because we're all counting on you.

One more thought: This book is the content of our hearts and minds. We have spent over three decades creating delightful user experiences. Our desire to improve ourselves and our work has been a constant thread. And just because we've deemed ourselves ready to share our expertise doesn't mean that our desire or our need for self-improvement has diminished. In other words, as proud as we are of this book, it is a snapshot, and as such will need to be improved over time as well. We'd love your thoughts, your feedback, your complaints, your nitpicks, and even once-in-awhile your compliments.

And for taking some of your valuable time to give our book a chance to have an impact on your work, you have our deepest appreciation and kindest wishes.

Hillel Cooperman
hillel@jacksonfish.com

Jenny Lam
jenny@jacksonfish.com

CHAPTER ONE

The Day Bill Gates Called Me Rude –
and Other Lessons in User Experience.

(A quick note: most of our book is written from our perspective. But this happened to Hillel so he tells this particular story.)

There was an almost interminable pause in the conversation, as Bill thought about what I had said. And then he looked up at me after some processing and exclaimed: "That's just rude."

~~~

In November of 2003 it was my job to get Bill Gates on board with the new designs my team had planned for the Windows user interface. I'd been in countless meetings with Bill, and already knew that I wasn't great at convincing Bill of much. When it came to discussing the user interface of Windows, we generally spoke past each other, which didn't make sense to me then, but makes a lot of sense to me now.

The currency of the software industry, an industry that Bill Gates helped create, is the engineer. Software gets built without executives, without marketers, without designers, and without accountants. It even gets built without testers. But it doesn't ever get built without engineers. Bill is the ultimate engineer. Back in the 1980's when graphical user interfaces were new and shiny, Bill internalized many of the lessons that made those original GUIs work. Concept reduction, consistency, skill portability, were all core to how to make a great UI. Why have 17 different ways to pop up (or drop down) a menu? Why have 17 different graphical treatments? With "one menu to rule them all," users could learn how to use the menu once and then apply this knowledge anywhere they saw this affordance. That way, developers don't have to reinvent the wheel, and users don't need to relearn the wheel.

And this is still a sound fundamental principle of user interface design.

But engineers (like everyone) see the world through their lens. Engineers look at code all day. And when they see two pieces of code doing roughly the same thing, they immediately think about ways they could eliminate the wasted effort by combining them into one piece of code that performs both functions. And often, when coders participate in UI design, they make the same observations, and can overdo this principle.

Additionally, though it's uncomfortable for the left-brained among us to discuss, another one of the fundamental aspects of today's state-of-the art user experience design is to focus on how the software makes the user 'feel'. You can imagine how popular a fuzzy notion like this is in a company (and industry) where empirically -minded engineers and their fans are running the show.

Just as I'd known it before all my previous meetings, I knew that Bill didn't love my fuzzy notions about what makes for a great user experience. I'll also confess at this point that I have a personal weakness when it comes to beautiful analogies. I overestimate their power to get people excited about ideas in which I'm invested. They're certainly effective, but perhaps not to the degree that I imagine.

Back to my meeting in the board room with Bill Gates, and the three or four executives between him and me in the Microsoft org chart. While the actual specifics of the day's discussion are lost to history, I do remember clearly that we were debating the merits of my team's user interface designs for powerful new data management features in the Windows Explorer. From my perspective, Bill's preferred direction was overly abstract. We had created a compact set of tools to help users manage their files and folders where we felt we'd balanced the "learning curve" that comes with anything new with the way human beings actually think about things. Bill felt that we could reduce the concepts much further, thereby easing each user's learning curve, and ultimately making them more powerful as they could employ this learning across a wide variety of scenarios. Cue my "beautiful" analogy.

At one particularly frustrating moment, I offered the following: "Bill, a shower, a toilet, and a water fountain all have mechanisms to control water flow, places where the water comes out, some sort of porcelain basin to hold the water, and a drain, but we don't combine them into one thing to reduce their learning curve. We don't merge them into one object because each of them are in use in fundamentally different ways at different times."

Then the pause.

Then Bill's verdict.

Ouch.

As I saw my career disintegrate before me, I started to question just how "beautiful" my analogy really was. To his credit, Bill was forgiving, and met with me many times after that, giving me numerous opportunities to get him on board with all manner of ideas coming from my team (with varying degrees of success on my part). The real lesson of the day was learned. In the software industry, as long as the engineering-minded run the show, the notion of subtle and textured user experience design that balances the emotional and functional aspects of a software experience will always struggle to take root.

Postscript: We all grow. Some of us have more capacity to do that than others. Bill Gates is certainly someone with massive 'capacity'. I was lucky enough to get to show my work to Bill again years later. And while he's still definitely an engineer at heart (which is a good thing), his depth and appreciation for some of the 'softer' aspects of a user experience have definitely evolved.

CHAPTER TWO

Software versus Content — The Lines Have Blurred

There was a time (and in some people's minds that time is still today) when people thought of software as a spreadsheet, or a word processor. Or in most cases, with normal human beings, software was something made by geeks that didn't really affect their lives in a day-to-day fashion. And even though those of us in the technology field know that software permeates and brings to life an increasingly larger percentage of the hardware we use every day, we have often treated software as a narrow silo rather than the unique, universal canvas it has become.

Historically technologists have viewed software as distinct from content. Software solves problems, it does stuff. Content is created by writers, musicians, filmmakers, et al. It is consumed. The narrative tells us that engineers create software to help those creative types create more content. They create software that authors, edits, displays, and shares that content, but the software itself is distinct from the content.

The dictionary is helpful in illustrating the out-of-date (and narrow) view:

soft·ware, [sawft-wair] –noun
General expression used to describe a collection of instructions enabling a computer to solve one or several tasks.

The first crack in this definition was the web itself. At first most people considered the web browser the software and web pages the content. But as web pages became more sophisticated in functionality, the distinction lost its usefulness. Compare Microsoft Excel vs. Google Spreadsheet:

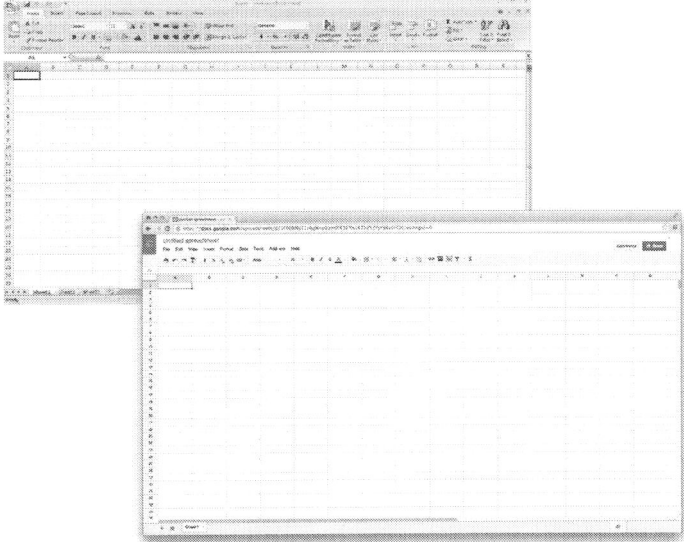

Even though designers have gotten more involved by virtue of the fact that many people feel web pages need to be "designed", unhelpful distinctions still exist. Let's look at another example: what's the difference between these experiences?

Or these:

Or these:

The movie isn't interactive while the game is. Does that mean the movie isn't software? The map and the video game are almost indistinguishable from each other. Newspapers are still printed on dead trees but they still have a user experience, and you can still interact with them.

Most software professionals are allergic to the techniques that are used to create compelling content. Content doesn't wake up in the morning thinking about how to be useful. Content isn't trying to solve a problem. Content is born to make you feel something — to elicit an emotional response. Content is trying to tell you a story. It is this purpose that needs to take its place alongside functionality and usefulness as core to every piece of software we create.

The line between software and content isn't just blurry, it's irrelevant. But its continued existence makes many technologists eschew the foundational design and storytelling techniques that are critical for making great user experiences.

CHAPTER THREE

Past is Prologue - What We Can Learn from Cars

In his autobiography "My Life and Work" (1922), Henry Ford remarked about the 1909 Model T that "Any customer can have a car painted any color that he wants so long as it is black."

While Henry Ford was painting his cars black, General Motors embraced the role of the designer in creating vehicles that were not only functional, but desirable. A key inflection point in the evolution of GM's thinking was the commissioning of Haley Earl to design a luxury car called the LaSalle for GM in 1927. After seeing the success of the car, Alfred Sloan, GM's president founded the "Art and Color Section" at General Motors. Earl was installed as the section's leader.

Up until this point, the body of the automobile was an afterthought for most American car manufacturers. Engineers focused on keeping costs low, and producing parts at volume. They optimized for the challenges of the engineering department and thought functionality was all they needed to provide to entice customers. Haley's new role at General Motors caused friction with other employees including executives and the engineers themselves. They thought Haley's designs were gratuitous. He was called one of the "pretty picture boys" and his department at the company was nicknamed "The Beauty Parlor".

In the culture of the United States in the late 1920's, is referring adult men as pretty, or their workplace as a "beauty parlor" a compliment? (Would it be intended as a compliment even today? We suppose that's another discussion entirely.)

In the late 1920's then market-leading Ford lost its sizable lead to Alfred Sloan's General Motors. The creation of the Art and Color department was another step in Sloan's product philosophy — a philosophy that valued the emotional aspect of the vehicle as much as the functional value. This contrast with Ford's stodgy designs played a significant role in GM surpassing Ford as the largest automobile manufacturer in the world.

Ultimately, all automobile manufacturers that survived made the transition to incorporate design as core to the DNA of how they make products. Technology companies are making that transition today.

Despite some notable exceptions (Apple), has the bulk of today's engineering driven software industry grown much beyond these statements of their spiritual forefathers at General Motors in the first half of the 20th century?

We believe the answer is emphatically "no".

It's important as you work within your own organization to recognize that some of your co-workers and management may still believe that functionality, or technical specs, will win the day. It's nor surprising given that improving the technology has won the day many times before. But disruptive leaps in technology don't come very often. In between those leaps, the battle for customers' hearts and minds will be won with design. Hopefully the story of the car industry will not only give ycu perspective on some of your co-workers, but may help them see what lies ahead as well.

CHAPTER FOUR

Software is Both Art & Craft

> *"You can be both a designer and an artist, a humanist and a*
> *technologist, a student and a teacher, a hand craftsman and a*
> *Photoshop guru, a global and local thinker..."*

–John Maeda, from his 2008 RISD Inauguration Speech

Despite the proliferation of technology, the creation of software is not a science. It's not an art either. If anything, software professionals mostly consider it a craft – something that requires skilled work. When it comes to design, most people in our industry think of design as art because it requires intuition as well as raw creative force.

Traditionally, software designers have viewed art as distinct from craft. Craft requires deep skills that are well executed and meet specific goals. Craft is about detailed execution and attention to detail, fit and finish.

Art, in the software designer's mind, is fuzzy, fluffy, and is primarily self expression. To do art and be an artist, you have to express something personal and have a distinct point of view or story that might be interpreted in various ways.

Scary!

Most of the software designers we encounter are allergic to thinking about their work as art. Is it because they worry they'll lose the tenuous respect of the engineers if they use fluffy terms like art and emotion? Let's take an example from the world of engineering. Not the engineering of digital products, but old school engineering. Let's take a moment to consider the Empire State Building.

The Empire State Building is the result of thousands of skilled craftspeople's hard work AND the building itself is an expressive piece of art. When you experience the Empire State building, without a doubt there is a visceral feeling you get from simply being in the space. There's grandeur and awe and excitement. The building is like a time-machine – it transports you to a period when American society expressed itself through stunning large-scale architecture. Of course every person who enters the building is affected in his or her own way, but there's no denying that it's the kind of experience that gets your heart pumping faster. And if you're even remotely inclined to admire creativity and craftsmanship, it can inspire you to make something amazing yourself.

We believe software has this same potential – to be crafted to serve the individual human being. For the person to experience the perspective of the product in a meaningful and emotional way.

When software is at its best, it is art *and* craft – where the design and construction of the product are intermingled to express a point of view with a purpose create a specific set of emotions and a personal relationship with the individual.

While many may debate the line between art and craft, blurring that line on purpose is the software imperative of the 21st century.

CHAPTER FIVE

A Very Short (and Incomplete) History
of Software User Experiences

If you're going to be an advocate of creating great user experiences, it is important to have your bearings — know what came before you.

Before the first Macintosh arrived in 1984, graphical user interfaces were in their infancy. Text interfaces were the norm. And consistency was nowhere to be found. Arcane commands and procedures ruled the day. And we liked it that way. It made us feel special that we knew how to view the file directory, and other people didn't.

Then the Macintosh arrived. A common interaction language for the core functions of software was its gift to our industry. Pointing, clicking. Windows, menus. Selecting and operating on selections. Icons. Folders. The metaphorical language as well as the guidelines telling you when to use what verb, which noun, set the stage for

Windows, and the next 10-15 years of software user interface development. The transformation was undeniable. Only the crustiest of technologists lamented the loss of their clubbiness and branded these new GUIs as for simpletons only.

For a decade… The icons got more colorful. The windows got bevelier (yes, we know that's not a real word). And the menus got overcrowded. But ultimately not much changed, until the web.

The web introduced new tools in our user interface arsenal — most importantly the hyperlink, the back button, and the ability to update software instantaneously (whether users liked it or not). The first two were important extensions of the core language introduced to the masses back in 1984 by the Mac. The third enlightened us that it didn't take months (or years) to improve a user interface. It could be done instantaneously — for everyone. But beyond these three the web gave us an additional gift — it smashed assumptions about the need for consistency.

Up until well-designed web pages appeared, user interface "experts" would rely primarily on consistency and rules to maintain quality. But the web was out of control. Anyone could make a web page, and did. And while lots of web pages were ugly, or hard to navigate, some were beautiful, compelling, and surprisingly simple. Users didn't retrain. They didn't need complex manuals. The web delivered user interfaces where the number of elements that needed to be consistent were much smaller than we'd been taught. And it didn't matter. The previous overly expansive focus on consistency now seemed foolish. (Hobgoblins, little minds, etc.)

This was more painful than you might think. Because the old guard was made up primarily of technologists. Technologists didn't just love consistency for consistency's sake, they loved it as it mirrored their understanding of the technology they were building from a code perspective. Engineers look to reduce the amount of code in their programs. They try to reuse pieces of code over and over in similar situations in their software. Similarly, engineers try to reduce the number of concepts in an app. The remaining concepts form a framework that they teach to the user. The thinking goes, once the user knows the framework, they can accomplish anything in the user interface. This isn't wrong so much as overdone. Humans don't always perceive very similar tasks as similar at all. Sometimes they need things to feel different even when an engineer's logic would dictate a more efficient path.

One of our favorite examples is the creation of a PDF. For many years (and still in some cases today) when you launch a word processor and want to save your document as a PDF, you don't choose "Save as…" from the File menu. Instead you choose "Print." Why is this the case? Because the way you actually create a PDF is by using the same kind of software (a print driver) that you would use to print a physical document. Why create a whole new place to access creating a PDF when the technical architecture of creating PDFs places the task right next to printing? In this way the user interface reflects the code underneath, and not necessarily the way humans think about it. Consistent? Yes. Accessible for most human beings? No.

But even scarier, it wasn't engineers that were creating all those inconsistent web pages, it was designers. And the engineers didn't do themselves any favors. Designers were learning HTML and CSS and created web pages without the help of an engineer. This was the beginning of the end of the engineering discipline's hegemony over the user interface.

The end result of the design vs. engineering conflict over user experience was never in doubt. The smart technologists switched sides and realized the benefits of the new approach. They became amateur designers, or professional ones in some cases. If they didn't opt to do the design themselves, they would recruit designers to join their teams. And ultimately, the combination of designers and technologists who saw the future started defining success as more than consistency but as usability. The seeds were planted in the early 90's, but the web accelerated the ability of people to design software around humans vs. the software being primarily a reflection of the code with which it was written. Human-centered design was here to stay.

New goals of discoverability, time-to-task, task completion, and more, gave us engineering-like metrics we could use to start to measure our software experiences. This was a great way to get the stragglers on board with the "new way". We could measure user response to our software in more scientific ways. We could tell you which user interface was better. Definitively. And this was good. Measuring how users interacted with software was and is good. And yet, something was missing.

In the 2000's two things happened. The first modern web browsers arrived with client-software-like user interface rendering capabilities. Second, high-powered mobile devices (like smartphones and tablets) arrived with powerful user interface rendering capabilities. Suddenly the main places users experienced technology had very powerful capabilities and engaging user interfaces. The designers had more tools at their disposal. But the complexity of these new platforms meant that the engineers had to be more involved.

But something else mattered also — brand.

The notion that software was an expression of the brand, the identity, the raison d'etre of a business, was new. It had been staring us in the face for years. For years people's opinions of Microsoft were formed by the multiple hours a day they sat in front of Windows (and much less so by the minutes per year they sat in front of Microsoft's advertising). This was true for every technology company. The user experience was core to the brand impression the company made. But this was invisible to many of the companies who created that technology. Apple had understood it for years, but (as usual) they were among the exceptions.

But just as big brands had heavily designed websites, they charged into apps with the same zeal for making a brand impression. When it was websites getting this treatment, the notion that software was a brand expression was dismissed. After all, "those websites are just ads. They're not really software. They don't do anything." Brands started creating apps that did things. Now it wasn't just the design that reinforced the brand, but the functionality itself that said something to the user about the company. Companies realized they could connect with customers by providing software as a service that actually did something. Not only was the fear of inconsistency a thing of the past, now it was imperative that your app actually stood out. It was imperative in a sense that your app be inconsistent.

Now that having software be desirable and creating an emotional connection with users were goals, how do you achieve those goals? Even if you built an app that was intuitive, appropriately consistent, measured high in usability tests, it might still leave users cold.

Today we must adhere to the lessons learned in the 1980's about appropriate consistency, the lessons learned in the 90's about updating our software regularly and not over-doing consistency, and ways to measure our effectiveness. And we must not forget those lessons all while we're absorbing the teachings of the new Millennium around how emotion and perception, the way customers feel about our software, will ultimately dictate how successfully our technology performs in the real world.

It's a lot to juggle, and yet, it's the state of our art.

CHAPTER SIX

Usability is the New Minimum Bar

The history of design naysayers in technological organizations is long and proud. We believe that we've evolved as an industry so that the notion of creating software that's usable has been socialized and mostly accepted. But crusaders like yourself will find themselves on a new front in the fight to create beautiful technology.

The new naysayer embraces usability, but decries visual depth. They push back on emotional connectedness. They focus on function to the exclusion of all but the barest of forms.

These are the people that would eat a piece of birthday cake and crow about its low price or ability to hold up the right number of candles, without recognizing that a slice of birthday cake not only tastes good – it can taste like childhood. It can transport you back to your own birthdays as a kid. You can relive that anticipation before you blow out the candles. Is that too much to ask from a birthday cake? Is that too much to ask of our software?

We're puzzled by the low bar among many software industry professionals. It seems that the highest aspiration for many software designers and technologists is to make their experiences "usable". Usable means many things, including simple, intuitive, and forgiving, to name a few. And these are important things.

But, to only make your software usable is like aspiring to make the food your restaurant serves just edible. Edibility, or rather, usability is the absolute baseline. And the fact that it often goes unachieved is great job security for software professionals. But it's not great for customers. It's the minimum. Perhaps there should be a software "health" inspector? "Why yes, it's true that I can use your software, but it's still not making me feel good."

The space beyond usability is the emotional experience of your software. What will your software say? How will it make your users feel? What are you saying? How are you making your users feel? Every time your user engages with your software they are reinforcing their feelings about you — the software's creator. Whether it's you personally, or your company, your user is building an impression of who you are. Your marketing, your name, your logo, your customer service all play a role, but the majority of time you spend with customers is through your technology.

What are we really talking about here? Your brand.

Your brand is not your logo. It's not your domain name. Or even your user interface. Your brand is the values that resonate with you and your customers. To put it more simply — your brand is comprised of the reasons you come to work every day. It's the passion and love that you pour into your software creation.

In our food analogy, your food experience should be about so much more than just being safe to eat. Frankly, it should be about more than it tasting good. The best dishes are the ones you remember. A meal you cherish and fondly reminisce about. A dish that conjures up positive emotions and memories. That's the food that you want to eat again and again.

And if you don't care about your creation with that kind of passion, your customers will know it. It can't be manufactured. It can't be faked. It's who you are.

Usability is the baseline. Your values, aspirations, and dreams are what fills the space above.

CHAPTER SEVEN

Branding User Experience

Brand ≠ Logo

The concept of branding is almost as misunderstood as the concept of user experience. A brand is not just the logo, or the visual identity or even the product. So what exactly is a Brand? Our favorite definition comes from Marty Neumeier's book, The Brand Gap. He says, "A brand is a person's gut feeling about a product, service, or organization." It's all about the aggregate perception.

For some reason when it comes to software, the division between brand marketing and user experience is a chasm. That's because traditional interface designers don't see brand as their job. Slap a logo on it and check off the brand box on the to-do list. When there's a disconnect between product experience and brand values, you've got a weak brand with no clear identity.

MailChimp, an email marketing service, does an exceptional job carrying its brand values throughout the experience. MailChimp is about having fun, being humorous, providing a powerful service that is easy, and delivering it in a casual (but still professional) way. These traits are not only visible in the visual identity and personified in the lovable mascot chimp, it's also in the behavior, tone and voice of the experience.

One example we love is how they handle user assistance. MailChimp encourages users to keep their e-mails appropriately narrow. The software uses a chimp's arm as a ruler to suggest email width. If you go too wide, the chimp's arm rips off! It doesn't get much clearer than that. Would users prefer that a dialog box popped up that said: "Exceeded maximum recommended e-mail width. Click OK to continue."? The Mailchimp team calls their approach "monkey love". It's a tiny (and infrequent) moment in the experience, and negative reinforcement at that, but it expresses their brand values, and how the user experience can deliver on those values. It's a moment where they deliver a brand experience that is useful, memorable, and fun.

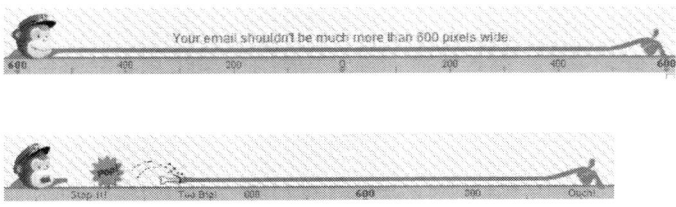

When the product experience, look & feel, tone & voice are aligned and delivered thoughtfully, your customers will start to build a coherent perception about your product/company. Once you've done that, congratulations! You have a built a strong brand.

Brand Touchpoints

That perception improves when the values of your brand are expressed in every interaction customers have with your product and your company. These include moments (or "touchpoints") such as signup, error pages, customer support calls, tweets, and even what your office interiors look like. The point is, all these different types of experiences reinforce your brand and that in turn creates something that people can trust. They trust your brand because they know what to expect.

Brands like Apple, Virgin, OXO, and Starbucks do more than create reliable and consistent experiences. They've built products that people believe are unique and they did it through the magic of design. They've combined usability with trust and emotion. Who doesn't want that?

Isn't this the Marketing Department's job?

This question touches on one of the biggest problems in building and stewarding brands in the software industry today.

The short answer: The outbound marketing, the messaging that customers get through ads and PR is the brand promise. The experience of buying, using, and maintaining the product delivers on that brand promise. These must be in complete harmony.

The longer answer: Brand is outside the engineering team at big companies. This is part of the problem. There isn't nearly enough collaboration on the brand. Designers often see their job as adhering to a brand style guide. What they don't realize is they are designing the biggest touchpoint users will have with their company and therefore need to understand brand is their job too.

In 2000, when we first started working on the Windows team at Microsoft, there were only quarterly updates from the Product team to the Brand Marketers. We were baffled by this. Didn't they need to know what experience we were planning for them to do the brand marketing? Didn't we need to see the marketing to make sure it was aligned with what the product would be? And why weren't they more involved in decisions like how the OS was going to greet the users every time they logged in? We fixed the organizational collaboration issue by creating a more formal, regular, and communicative relationship with the marketing team. We still see organizational disconnects happen far too often. It can be difficult to manage a multi-disciplinary team of brand stewards but it can be done and the results are worth it.

Hopefully your job is much easier if you're at a smaller company where the Brand Marketing folks or Product folks are a little more accessible. For the sake of the brand and the people using your product, get together and collaborate.

Whether you work at a large company or a small company, you'll need to traverse organizational boundaries to get consensus on the core values of your product, your company, and ultimately define the DNA of your brand. Some might say that this is in fact the hard part. And we would agree. It is. But we were surprised at how many companies didn't even get to this part of the discussion. In our experience, getting the organization to see that having a multi-disciplinary approach to defining these experiences is important will immediately expose cracks in the facade. Engineering thinks one thing and marketing another? The surest way to find out is to force them to work together.

While the tactics you'll need to traverse some of those chasms could fill an entire additional book (and as such aren't listed here), we'll leave you with this thought: If the differences between team members aren't bridged and fashioned into a shared set of values, your organization has very little chance of connecting with your audience in a coherent and long-lasting way.

CHAPTER EIGHT

The Dark Art of Defining Success in User Experience Design

The technology industry is dominated by engineers. Logic and reason are the tools they love best. This makes sense as programming is essentially a logical puzzle. However, when it comes to user experience, these tools are not ideal. When software is slow, we measure its speed, the amount of memory it uses, as well as other metrics, and make changes until it conforms to our definition of success. This is straightforward and makes sense. And when it comes to specific user experience problems (e.g. users are deleting things by accident, users can't find this button, etc.) the same approach can be effective. Identify the problem in specific terms. Measure the baseline performance of the UX, propose changes, test changes with a representative audience sample, measure, iterate, deploy.

Done and done.

The problem comes when we are designing v1 products or doing major redesigns of existing things. With these broader design efforts there are so many factors at play that measurements become a muddle. Let's take a simple example and see just how complicated it can be to understand the results:

Let's say company X has two goals in redesigning their software. In the first goal they'd like to increase the engagement of their customers with their product. They measure engagement based on page views, minutes spent on the site, etc. Their second goal is to streamline the clunky user interface for the main functions of their software. To solve these problems, the software designers create a new polished streamlined user experience with some new features designed to pique the user's interest. Sounds good, right?

The new version of the software is rolled out and what happens? Engagement goes down. Are the new "engaging" features failing or did the streamlining eliminate a bunch of wasted page views and time on the site that users used to waste in the old clunky design? Perhaps if we measured exactly how much time was wasted in the old design we could compare that to the differences we're seeing and the remaining change would give us an indication of whether the new features are having any impact.

It would also be helpful to measure specific user interaction with just the new features. That will give us some sense of the true picture. But in the meantime, the overall engagement numbers are way way down, and the subtleties of these tradeoffs are lost in the discussion with the CEO and the CFO who are not happy. Furthermore, the deadline and constrained resources for the project means that the analytics code that needed to be written to measure the effectiveness of the new features never actually got done. But wait… there's more.

A small percentage of the site's users are complaining. Loudly. About the redesign. The "streamlining" moved some things around and they are pissed off. What percentage of the user base do they represent? It's impossible to know. Half a percent? Ten percent? Would you piss off ten percent of your users to make the other 90% way happier? Which ten percent did you anger – the most valuable customers or least valuable? Do you even have the tools to measure that? Are they leaving the service or just venting? Oh yeah, the press could go either way. They may love it. Or hate it. Or ignore it altogether. And it's not clear their opinion is anything other than ranting or has any impact on your potential customers making purchase decisions.

It gets complicated.

Some companies solve this problem by measuring overall customer satisfaction, or financial metrics. These methods don't validate the design changes individually, just the bigger picture, which frankly is ultimately the point of the design in the first place. And when it comes to a new product there's no previous version against which you can compare.

What's a company to do?

Should they trust the UX practitioners to not screw it up too badly? Listen to their gut instincts? Spend weeks or months coming up with elaborate mechanisms and schemes to measure the things that can be measured? (You'd be surprised how much money, time, and energy is often wasted in this pursuit because some software executive won't accept the degree of ambiguity involved in these broad stroke design efforts.)

We believe there are three things that help you feel good (and responsible) when it comes to major new design work:

1) Acceptance. Understand that the factors in success are often too complicated to specify, and some things you won't be able to measure as you would like.

2) Big Picture Perspective. Focus on the bigger picture around customer satisfaction, getting good reviews from press, customer testimonials, and the excitement of your own employees. (Don't underestimate this. Having a great design can do wonders for morale.)

3) Focus on the Few. Apply greater resources to fewer areas. And where you can get specific, do so. The screen on which you ask for money is a great place to get very specific about measurement, conversion rates, and do lots of iterative testing.

In a world of fast iteration, small teams, and constrained resources, the industrial strength testing and measurement efforts required to even shed light on a fraction of the mechanics involved in the success or failure of a broad user experience design effort are simply not realistic for most projects. In short, you can measure far fewer things than you would imagine. And even when you do measure, the data often raises more questions than it answers.

Executives at companies large and small don't like it when questions have fuzzy answers. It makes them feel like people aren't really trying. And some engineers are all too happy to tell them that UX design can be reduced completely to a science. But reality is messy. Once you accept that, you can focus on a few things that matter, and not get distracted by the broader set of things that are simply harder to know.

CHAPTER NINE

On Luck

The shelves of your now closed local bookstore, and the virtual shelves of your thriving online bookstore are filled with books that promise to tell you how to do something — create a successful business, hire the right people, get a great job, and in this case, get your high-tech organization to lead with design.

The single most important factor in success that almost none of these books write about is — luck.

It's not just that nobody writes about luck, it's that nobody acknowledges how big a role luck plays in success. Would you be discouraged if you found out that despite doing your best work, despite being better than everyone else, that without luck you would fail? What percentage of success depending on luck would be discouraging for you? 25%? 50%? 75% or more? Would you be discouraged? Would you give up?

There's no way to quantify what percentage of success is based on luck. We suspect that luck is upwards of 75% responsible for most success.

However, you don't win the lottery if you don't buy a ticket. Designing beautiful, intuitive, and standout software buys you lots of tickets to the lottery. You still need to get lucky, but when it comes to the things you can influence, you'll be doing your best. And while we can't guarantee success, we can guarantee that when you're done you'll be proud.

CHAPTER TEN

What it Means to Be a User Experience Designer

Here's an observation that will offend many people. It is easier for someone who's curious, has an eye for detail, some Photoshop chops, and good taste to learn interaction design than for a software person to learn how to do great aesthetics and presentation. To put it simply, becoming an "interaction designer" is really not that hard.

If you ask us to create a true software designer from either a) a smart and talented graphic designer, or b) a smart and talented interaction designer, nine times out of ten we will start with the graphic designer because the interaction design skills are much easier to acquire. From our perspective, while there are some interaction designers out there who certainly add value, there are a lot more who are essentially valueless.

And the perverse irony is people with the easily acquired skill who spend their time acting like graphic designers are a dime a dozen. We've seen many interaction designers referring to designing the presentation layer as "applying lipstick" or dismissing this stage as "something we can do later". In fact, the aesthetics need to come from a process where a true user experience designer is involved in crafting his or her vision from day one. Great design comes from teams where a user experience designer is informed enough to make technology choices to enable the experience they're trying to create; from teams where a UX designer is the person on the team who is ultimately responsible for having and executing on a vision for the kind of experience that the customer will encounter.

A true user experience designer is like a singer/songwriter. They can both write the music and perform it well. A great singer will fail singing a badly crafted song. And a poor singer will fail singing even the most beautiful composition. In the case of software design, scenario definition, interaction design, and basic structure are like songwriting. The song performance is the top-most layer of the user interface, the combination of images (still and moving), text, and audio that bring the experience to the users input mechanisms – sight, touch, sound (no smell and taste quite yet). And while it's true that you can find a great singer and a great songwriter to partner to create magic, unless you've found a partnership of true equals, one side tends to dominate the other. The majority of genuine artists both craft and perform their art.

When it comes to software, our industry's penchant for specialization is in full effect. The software designer's role is divided across an organization including the graphic designer, the information architect, the product manager, the usability engineer, the technical writer, the interaction designer, and in some cases the ethnographer. That's not to say that there aren't talents in every one of these roles. But in a world where small teams make great things, one good user experience designer can handle the vast majority of these tasks, and the result will be better than with the broader group.

In most software companies the roles are divided into two. The first role is what we'll call "interaction designer" which is everything except for drawing the actual art that goes on the screen. The "graphic designer" is hired for the rest. And in almost every organization, the interaction designer is in charge. This is backwards. We believe that most of the self-proclaimed "interaction designers" or "user experience architects" are a dime a dozen.

Not only should you have a true user experience design leader in your organization, but the organization should be built to serve the needs of that person. We're sure there are other ways to approach this problem. And there are certainly plenty of customers who don't appear to notice quality when it comes to product design (note all the customers of Wal-Mart and the Post Office). But more and more we think people (rightly) want to emulate VW and Apple. And we believe the only way to do this is to put a true software designer in charge. More on that in the next chapter.

CHAPTER ELEVEN

Why Does Silicon Valley Want Designers That Can Code? Because the Valley Doesn't Understand What Designers Do.

Jared Spool, a regular industry speaker and author on the topics of usability and software design, wrote a blog post titled "Why the Valley Wants Designers that Can Code". He makes the good point that managers at startups are always looking for ways to get more value for their dollar. He recommends "If you're a designer, you don't have to learn to code. But if you do, and you get good at it, you'll find more opportunities." And he's right. But his comments would be just as valid if he wanted "marketers that can code" or "engineers that can write press releases". Or any other combination of useful skills.

Except, Silicon Valley doesn't want marketers to write code or engineers to write press releases. They don't trust marketers to write code, and they feel that writing press releases would be a waste of the engineers' valuable time and skills.

What's the real reason that many companies look for designers who can code? Because fundamentally they don't understand and don't properly value what great software designers do.

Spool says: "If you're in a room filled with designers, bring up the topic of whether it's valuable for a designer to also code.

Immediately, the room will divide faster than Moses split the Red Sea. One side will tell you coding is an essential skill, while the other will vehemently argue how it dilutes the designer's value." If we're in a room full of designers and any of them take either of these positions, then we're in a room full of designers we would prefer never to work with.

Great software designers are true singer-songwriters. They deliver an interaction and visual design that don't just make a product shine, they define the product. They create its essence, its DNA. Should they have deep empathy for the software development process? Yes. Should they understand technology and be "technical" to a degree? Yes. Should they have passion for software as their medium? Yes. Much like a designer focused on print projects should understand how various ink/paper/press combinations will impact their final product's design as well as cost, software designers should understand the canvas on which they are painting. But do we want a true software designer spending time fighting the various inconsistencies between browser CSS implementations to get the UI perfect? Nope. It's a waste of their time. They should be doing more designing.

(If you're annoyed by the previous paragraphs, this next one will make you crazy.)

Are there true singer-songwriter software designers that can write high quality code? Yes. But they are the exception. Anecdotally, we've found that most "designers" who can code are in fact coders who have empathy and passion for design, and may even have some good interaction design chops. But often they are weak when it comes to visual design. In our left-brain dominated industry, visual design is looked at as fluff. Often people will say things like "art is the last step" or "that's the lipstick". We believe when you treat the visual elements as a layer of paint, then all the visuals can be is a layer of paint.

The worst part is that design schools are often complicit in this misunderstanding of what software designers should do. They're busy teaching HTML, CSS, and Flash (yes Flash) to art students as if these skills are mandatory for them to succeed. These potentially talented software designers have an allergic reaction to spending their careers writing markup instead of drawing and decide to focus on "print"! Print! Like calendars. Letterhead. Flyers. Annual reports. Taking ink and arranging it artfully on dead trees. The most incredible canvas in the world for designers — software — exists, and needs them. It lets them combine text and images and video and audio and user interaction in incredible ways, but they want to go make business cards and annual reports. Our industry needs thousands of talented software designers and design schools are failing to produce them.

Soon we will have more than a smattering of true software designers in this industry. They wont be employees either. They'll be founders and co-founders. And their companies will produce beautiful usable products that stand out from their competitors. And some of these designers will even be able to code. But we won't let them, because we'll want them spend every minute designing beautiful software.

CHAPTER TWELVE

Designer vs. Engineer –
The Curse of Low Expectations

We were sitting at a dinner. The dinner was for speakers at a design conference. We were among the speakers. Across from us sat another speaker. A software developer with an appreciation for beautifully designed software. This in itself is a good thing. You can have beautiful architectural plans but if the contractor has no appreciation for detail, then the plans won't get executed with care and live up to the vision.

Now, this analogy in itself is a problem as most software developers don't consider themselves akin to contractors. They think they are the architects as well. And this in fact was the discussion that ensued — what is the role of the user experience designer?

The enlightened engineer across the table lectured us on how important it was to have great designers — both interaction designers and visual designers on his project. We countered that those two tasks really should be relegated to one person. We added that it was difficult to be great at only one and really be a user experience leader on the team. The engineer responded that this was simply not realistic and told us that even if designers could do both interaction and visual design, they weren't technical enough to contribute to the project as peers much less as leaders.

We asked for an example.

The developer told us that a designer had proposed a web page's user interface to him that was laden with multiple megabytes of graphics for a web page that needed to load with lightning speed. This was his proof that the designer wasn't "technical" enough.

That was our proof that his designer was lousy.

Knowing about how the size of graphics affects load time is as technical an issue to understand as knowing the difference between requiring black and white vs. four color printing on a physical print design project. In other words, it's basic. As we've said before, designers don't need to know how to operate the press but they do need to know the basics of how it works and the constraints under which they work.

The engineer was stunned. His expectations were so low that it didn't occur to him to expect more of a designer. It didn't occur to him that a designer who uses Adobe's complicated products, deals with technology all the time, and understands file sizes, should be expected to take a web page's load time into account in their design.

Who's at fault? Is it the designer who's not thinking holistically about the project or the engineer who has such low expectations? The answer is: yes.

We have witnessed many user experience designers who partner closely with engineers. The engineer thinks creatively about how to get the design built to deliver on the emotional impact intended by the designer, and the designer thinks creatively about how to tweak their design so it's not only easy for the engineer to implement but to maintain as well. These are the collaborations we have enjoyed most. And all they require is a designer who has an appreciation for the medium of software as well as empathy for the realities of the development process, and an engineer with attention to detail who loves making beautiful software that customers love.

When this partnership is humming, fantastic user experiences are the result. When engineers think they themselves are the designers, and the actual designers conform to the engineers low expectations, the results are almost always disappointing.

So what about that sub-optimal situation?

What should you do as a designer if you don't have an engineering partner who brings you into the process? We'd love to point you to a detailed chapter with a seven-step program for growing your development partner into a true peer and collaborator, but the truth is much simpler, and unfortunately, much less reassuring. Developers are usually either inclined to want to make a beautifully designed product, or not. And if they're not, your images, your designs, and the words you put around them are your best shot at changing their minds. But if an engineer is intransigent, and the two of you are philosophically unaligned, then you really don't have any options. You can fight for scraps, or you can try and find a new situation. We realize that's not always possible, but unfortunately it may be the only answer available in some situations.

What should you do as a developer who wants a productive partnership? The best thing you can do is reward a good designer by building the designs they create with a careful and fastidious attention to detail. Designers love engineers who bring their designs to life while respecting even the minute details of the drawings. The other thing you can do is trust your designer. We understand that you may have spent many years being wholly responsible for the user interface of the software you code. But you're lucky that you now have someone who went to school, not to write code, but to create amazing designs that solve real user problems. Let them do their job, and yours will get even easier and more enjoyable. And if your designer is not up to the task, don't do it for them, push them to step up and exceed expectations. You might be surprised at what they do when pressed. For many designers nobody ever expected them to deliver anything beyond something "pretty". Expect more from them, and they might expect more from themselves.

CHAPTER THIRTEEN

Designer vs. Marketer – A Partnership Opportunity

The best designers are never satisfied. There are always more customer needs to meet. More problems to solve. More rough edges to polish. The perfect is the enemy of the good and yet every great designer knows you eventually have to ship. And preferably sooner rather than later. But the vision of how completely you want to tell the story of your product never shrinks. It only grows. And telling that story is your job as a designer, but it's almost never your job alone. That can be challenging, but it can also be good?

Customers hear your story from articles in the press, from friends' recommendations, from advertisements, and from trying the product themselves. Every interaction tells your story. And the marketer in your organization is typically responsible for all the storytelling beyond the product itself. The brand, the ads, the tone, all these things that the marketer is responsible for make up the promise. They are out there every day making promises to the public. In the best world the marketers and the designers/engineers are thick as thieves. The promise is something they came up with together. The marketers hone the story and the product folks hone the product itself. That product is the delivery of the promise made by the marketing. The promise and the promise's fulfillment go hand in hand. And they should be conceived from the same genetics. But that's not reality in many organizations.

Reality is something more along these lines.

Situation A – Marketing Rules the Roost
In these organizations, marketing defines the product, and the ads, and then tells the product/engineering folks what to create. They involve the product folks early on, but the product folks are the tail and the tail does not wag the dog in these organizations. In fact, the bulk of the design talent (if not all of it) is over in the marketing group. The engineers are relegated to strictly technical roles.

Situation B – Engineers are the Currency of the Realm
In these organizations, typically high-tech companies, the engineers are kings. Everyone else is second class. Ultimately the engineers write the code and thereby decide what the product will be. Do YOU want to argue with that surly engineer who's worked here for 20 years and written 80% of the codebase by himself? (And yes, it's almost always a "him".) The designers are also-rans in this organization. The marketers are there to dress up whatever the engineers deliver. Sometimes the marketers generate many documents trying to convince the engineers what to build. This rarely works.

Designers have the opportunity to rise above this dichotomy by taking the initiative and partnering intelligently. In a previous chapter we talked about how designers can partner with engineers who want to make great products. In high-tech companies where the marketers have limited say over the product, the designers can become their biggest advocate even if the engineers are keeping marketing out of the process.

Situation C – The Dream
In this world the product designers partner with the marketers from day one. They collaborate on the story they want to tell the customers. Assuming that they have already done the heavy lifting of carving out a meaty role for themselves on the product team (see the previous chapter), the designers should have enough leverage in the engineering organization and technical know-how that they know what can and can't be built in a reasonable timeframe with the technology available. The marketers bring the product people into the brand and advertising discussions (usually strictly marketing's own domain) as they know that these things need to be designed together. The logo is not something to be jammed in an empty rectangle on the screen the day before the product launches. (We've seen this happen firsthand.) The brand, the identity, the tone of the language, the aesthetics, the collateral visual elements, even the audio cues all tell a singular story and comprise a shared toolbox that the marketing department and the user experience designers pull from. And in this world, the promise and the delivery of that promise are harmonious. Also – flying cars.

This doesn't guarantee success, but it's better than a promise unkept, or a great product never discovered because of a lousy promise.

Marketers in situation A are less likely to want to partner to this degree because they only have things to lose. They're already in charge. But in high-tech companies, the opacity of the engineering process leaves marketers as peripheral players in the politics of building the product. That's where a designer has an opportunity to insert themselves. In many of these companies the marketers' only sense of impact is in how much budget they have to spend on the marketing of the product (be it for research or outward bound messaging). Designers who understand this dynamic and are willing to take on some of the marketers' work on the side will have the advantage in bridging the divide and creating The Dream situation. You heard me right... do design favors for the marketers. They have limited budget and much of it is spent hiring people THAT ARE ALSO DESIGNERS. Do some design work for them on the side and they will be your best friends.

Ultimately, as with partnering with engineers, you've either got some material to work with or you don't. Some marketers will be excited about the partnership. Some will not. Some will realize the overall value, and some will be defensive. As usual, you can take your best shot at trying to convince them to be true partners by showing them your work and getting them to buy into the notion of defining the vision together. Pictures are often so much more convincing than words. That said, there will be people who don't want to partner. And in those cases, you may not be able to realize this dream.

To even have a chance though, user experience designers must speak the language of marketers. They must understand the dynamics of their business, and the metrics used to measure the business' success. In other words, the designer must not only embrace the technology of their medium but the economics of it. The designer that can straddle those worlds and deliver designed solutions that factor in both sets of requirements into a product that people love is the true User Experience Design Leader.

CHAPTER FOURTEEN

Designer vs. Product Manager —
The Turf Battle

It must be the goal of every aspiring User Experience Designer to eliminate the need for Product Managers who do anything other than outbound marketing. The need for someone to go-between the marketer and the engineer is over. User Experience Designers worth their salt should be performing this role, and running rings around Product Managers. An MBA from Wharton, or a CS degree from Stanford does not qualify you to understand customers as human beings and design end-to-end experiences that make them happy. This is not to say there aren't some great design-focused MBAs and CS majors. But they are the exceptions, not the rule.

In the early days of software development, designers were rare. And even when they were involved, it was in spot roles like icon creation, or logo fashioning. There wasn't awareness of the role a user experience designer could play because there were no such people.

It was obvious, that left to their own devices, many software engineers made terrible user interfaces. There were exceptions. Design-minded engineers would not only make great user interfaces but invented the very language of user interfaces that we use today. But for most engineers a little help was in order. Thus was born the role of the Product Manager. (In some companies this role is sometimes called Program Manager). And in some companies there are Program Managers and Product Managers (and even Project Managers) dividing the roles even further.

Generally, responsibilities for folks in the "PM" role often include some combination of:

- Understand the customer and the market.
- Define the functionality of the software.
- Shepherd the project to completion on time and on budget.
- Outbound marketing.

These are important tasks, and they need to be done. But the modern User Experience Designer is encroaching on this space quickly and the Product Managers aren't happy about it. To truly have a holistic view, a user experience design leader must understand their customer and market as well as define the functionality of the software. Design is not about putting a veneer on top of some functionality that's already been created. Design is about creating a holistic package that delights the customer. Design is about understanding what plumbing needs to exist so the ultimate customer experience can match expectations. And good user experience design leaders are stepping up in this role.

What's left for the Product Manager? Essentially project management and outbound marketing. As for project management, this is a thankless task that should be performed by whoever controls the engineering resources. They are the ultimate contractor getting the project built and should be doing resource management and planning. As for the outbound marketing, a quality user experience design leader will be involved in this as well making sure that the marketing materials are a holistic extension of the user experience. Actually to be more accurate, a design leader will recognize that the marketing materials ARE part of the UX and treat them accordingly. Ultimately the marketing is a promise that the software itself needs to deliver on. It only makes sense that one person would oversee everything from the promise to the promise-keeping.

When you see a company where the role of product definition is performed by someone other than a user experience designer, this is a comment on the state of the profession as a whole. If you are a Product Manager, it's your job to groom a crop of talented User Experience Designers to take your job. And if you're a User Experience Designer, you need to compete for that role by stepping up and showing your mettle.

If we want to live in a world where most of the software created makes us feel the care, and thought, and love that were put into it, then helping designers earn their way into these roles is a mission we should all share.

CHAPTER FIFTEEN

Why We Won't Hire People Who Want to Be the "User Advocate" on the Development Team

Periodically we see mail from people looking for a job. Often it's more of a general call for work rather than a specific request for work at our little startup. And often, the people who are calling for work declare their undying passion for user-centered design. They go on to talk about how understanding the user is the most important factor in creating great software, and how vociferous their support is of said user during the development process.

We don't care what your role is. Everyone should be a user advocate. Everyone should have a common bar for the caliber and quality of the software the team is delivering. Everyone should understand what it means for their end product to be "on brand". And everyone should be able to balance that with the realities of the business and software development.

Declaring yourself as the "user advocate" can lead to four difficulties:

- It assumes the worst case by default – nobody else on the team is a user advocate (which of course they should be).
- It assumes that you come into the team better at something than any of your new teammates. (Likely, you don't.)
- It absolves you of other responsibilities and perspectives on the team (or at the very least gives others the impression that you've absolved yourself).
- And worst of all, it can absolve other team members of being user advocates in their own right. Until every member of an organization is focused on the end-to-end customer experience of a product, whether it's delivering software or pizza, the experience is never going to be great.

We recognize many software development teams are still technology rather than customer-focused. We also recognize that many of the teams who declare themselves "user-focused" are no such thing at all at least in practice. When someone declares their passion for users as a software developer it's like humans declaring their passion for oxygen. Yeah, we're all big fans.

CHAPTER SIXTEEN

Put the Designer in Charge

A note: We recognize that many of the people reading this book are likely not in charge or in a position to be in charge just yet. However, we know that for up and coming design talent with a penchant for leadership, this is an argument they will need to make. So below we'll outline the case for putting the designer in charge of the end-to-end experience of the product including the resources that build it, support it, and tell its story.

The most important thing you can learn about an organization is who they decide to put in charge.

When we choose a leader, since no one person is ever completely well-rounded or expert in every task necessary, we end up picking people who are better at some things than others. Some groups pick leaders who are the best at doing the primary function of whatever it is that group does. Some groups pick leaders who are the best at leading – often generalists. But invariably, the choice of a leader is making a statement about the identity of the organization. Not just in terms of that person's style, but also in terms of what skillset they think is most important.

In software companies, there are two types of people that get put in charge. Engineers, and marketing/business folks. Sometimes a salesperson will sneak through but that's typically an exception.

These choices were fine when the software industry was immature. But as we enter this new age, these choices are no longer appropriate. The goal of a technology company isn't to write code. It's not to create marketing messages. It's not even to make money. That's right. The goal is not to make money. Ask your employees and co-workers why they're there. If the only reason is to make money, and not because they're passionate about some higher goal, then find a new company because your company will have a very difficult time making something great. Money is what's necessary to run a successful business, but it's not the goal.

The goal of the modern, enlightened, forward-thinking technology company should be to create a user experience that is indispensable, delightful, memorable, useful, and special. That's it. And frankly, it should be the overarching goal of any company creating any service or product, but we'll stay in our realm of expertise — the world of software.

And since the goal is creating this incredible user experience, it's fitting that the person in charge has as his or her fundamental expertise – creating amazing user experiences. Some companies call this a "product person". Call it whatever you want. But it's the person who ultimately sweats every detail of how the company and the company's products and services interact with its customers. From every pixel in the software, to the headline on the ad, to the way the customer support person answers the phone. This is the person who needs to be in charge. And this person needs to have deep expertise in the broadest sense when it comes to the discipline of design.

Having a UX designer on staff is not enough. Having a UX designer be your VP of design is not enough. Don't make them argue with the engineers over resources. Don't waste his or her time arguing with marketing over the logo. Put this person in charge over the end-to-end experience. Not just how the product looks, but what the product does.

We acknowledged at the beginning of this chapter that our message here is not necessarily for the likely customer of this book, but rather for their boss (or their boss' boss' boss.) That said, let's address that boss right now. Directly.

Hi Boss. We know this is a bit of a stretch for you. What will the engineers think? What will the sales people think? The marketing people will freak out. What does someone who knows how to use Photoshop know about business? It is your job as the big boss to grow your stellar design talent into stellar overall leaders. Design is about problem solving. Leadership is about problem solving. We don't believe that every designer can be a leader, but we know that most leaders can't suddenly become experts at design. Putting a leader with a design background in charge of your organization makes a statement to everyone in the organization about the importance of the customer experience. If that's not a statement to which you're prepared to pay more than lip service, you should ask yourself just how important having an end-to-end polished customer experience truly is.

A couple of other thoughts:

If you don't have a designer that can do that job, than you don't have a true User Experience Design leader in your organization. (See *Chapter 17: How to Hire a Designer.*)

If you're a designer who isn't ready to step up and do that job, then you're not a true User Experience Design leader. At least not yet. *(See Chapter 19: Turning Yourself Into a User Experience Design Leader.)*

CHAPTER SEVENTEEN

How to Hire a Designer

If you look back about ten years, the designer was effectively non-existent on most software teams. If you were working on a large project, there was perhaps one designer to every 50-100 engineers who worked on icons or just the graphical interface. But thankfully, that's changed. It's moving in the right direction due to how the engineering discipline and tools have evolved and how software products are trying to be more user-centered. Today, there's enormous demand for great product design leadership in every software team.

Even the most enthusiastic engineering managers are still stymied because it's really challenging to find GREAT designers. The demand is outpacing the talent. And engineers and MBAs who are looking for that leadership have almost no experience in evaluating or hiring for design.

Can I get by without a designer? Or at least hire a designer later?

If you want to create a product that stands out and connects with people, hire a designer. Not just any designer. A great one who can lead and who you can trust. Waiting too late to hire hurts your chances of finding one that's invested and passionate about the product. It's harder to convince a designer to come in midstream to clean up a mess than to ask a designer to come create an amazing product with you. Designers are no different than engineers in this respect.

Before you begin your design search...

Many of you reading might not be a CEO. But you may be in a position where you're trying to convince your CEO (or other company leader of your position). Here's an argument for you to use: If you're a CEO, it's important to get introspective and ask yourself "What kind of CEO are you?" Starting your own company is sort of like jumping out of a plane. Scary, dangerous, exhilarating. So, are you the kind that packs her own parachute before jumping out of a plane? Because you want to be accountable for that parachute that will save your life. Or are you the kind of CEO that gets the professional parachute packer down the street to pack your parachute. He's been packing parachutes for 10-15 years and does this for a living. Hiring a design lead means hiring someone you trust to make big decisions.

What does it take to be a great design leader?

Being great at capital 'D' Design comes with many years of experience. And there are many skills, from user research, product strategy, visual design, interaction design, copywriting, human factors, prototyping, information architecture, usability, to broad understanding of engineering and technical issues, etc. But no one can do everything.

It's far too common to see a job description like this:

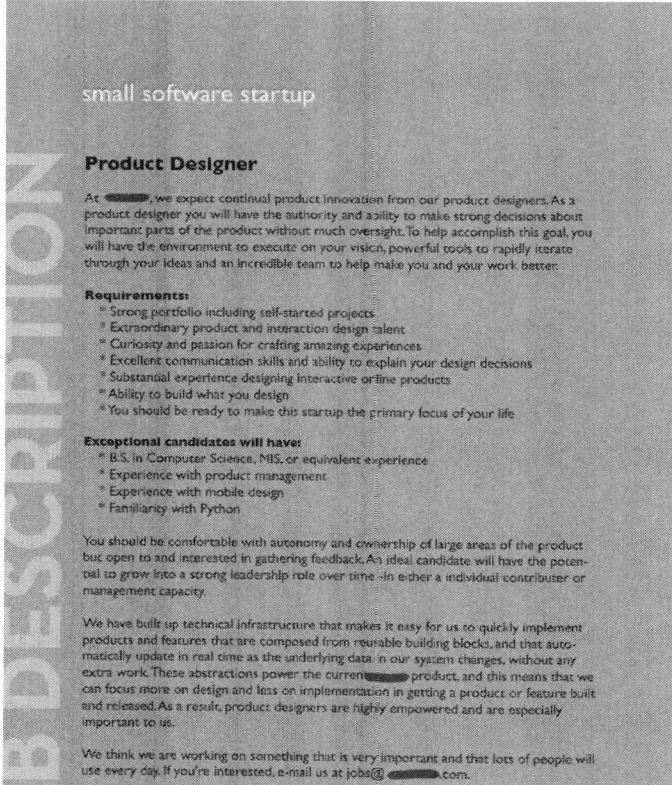

It's OK to aim for a designer who can do it all. But realistically, designers who say they can design and code are usually not great at both.

The primary skills a designer needs to have expertise in are: visual design and interaction design. Sure they need to understand what the user's needs and goals are (user research), how the product fits the needs of the business model (product design). In a world of smaller teams, all those skills are part of the job, not specialized roles.

~~~

The Design Hire Checklist:

- Formal design training: degree in communications design, product design, or human computer design engineering. They should be design fluent – meaning they can speak to technical design principles when discussing a design.

- Well-designed online portfolio with well-designed work (While it begets a chicken-and-egg problem you may need to hire a designer to help you evaluate other designers. Sometimes it can be a senior consultant who you couldn't afford for the entire job, but who you can use to help you find someone who is a full-time fit):

- The work should be large screens or links to the live design. If they only show small thumbnails, it might be that they are trying to hide something.

- Every piece should be great. Any duds in the portfolio reflects poor judgment. Investigate why they decided to put that piece in the portfolio.

- How the portfolio is designed is a big clue to how they think about interaction design. Is the navigation intuitive? Is it easy to to see more details on a project? Is the information architecture clear? Are the calls to action obvious?

- Passionate about technology: it helps if the designer is a bit 'nerdy' (in the best sense of the word) and likes to tinker with technology. This is a good sign that they have a lot of empathy and respect for the other side of the product development team.

- Have shipped something: there's no substitution for going through an entire ship cycle. Because many designers come out of the agency world where they are so cut off from the actual development and execution of a product, there can be unrealistic expectations of the kind of trade offs designers have to make throughout the development process.

- Amazing attitude: This is the most important factor on top of talent. Design is not as measurable as engineering and the work relies much more on innate creativity which is mostly subjective. This can get to an emotionally vulnerable place where the designer needs a mature and steady attitude to deal with potentially emotional feedback from the team and from users. If you got someone who has an attitude that is curious, positive, humble, and continuously eager to grow, you really can't go wrong.

The Interview

Everyone has their own process for the interview loop that works for them but when it comes to the designer there's just one piece of advice I have – unless you are a senior designer yourself, you should always enlist the help of a senior design leader (possibly using a friend you respect from another company, or hiring a senior UX consultant) to participate in the interview process. This is especially important when it comes to evaluating the work in his/her portfolio. Senior designers who have been around the block have an eye for well-executed, thoughtful design and a BS detector. They can help figure out exactly what part of the design the interviewee was accountable for and they can also uncover the designer's center of gravity.

CHAPTER EIGHTEEN

I Can't Find a True User Experience Design Leader for My Company. What Do I Do Next?

At this point, you're hopefully in agreement on the importance of having a true User Experience leader in charge of your design, and most likely of your entire product. It's really easy for us to beat the drum on this point. What's harder is to find a human being who actually fits the bill.

There are many reasons for this:

- Design schools are simply not producing these people consistently. Designers are coming out of school with a focus on print or illustration or web development or interaction design. They're not being produced as well-rounded product/ UX people ready to lead you to victory.
- Our industry tends to relegate design folks to tactical responsibilities. "Please put lipstick on this pig. Thanks." So even great designers have a hard time breaking out of their little areas and leading the rest of the organization.
- Design can't be taught overnight. The folks in charge usually have a technical or sales/marketing background. And while this can be good it's not enough. And frankly, for many people

without taste, it's simply not teachable. Taste is not a skill one can typically acquire.

- Your project is too small, or not exciting enough to get anyone with the skills you need to work on it full time. High-end product design talent is hard to come by. And these folks have their pick of projects. If yours seems boring, the odds of getting them to make it their full-time job are very low.
- Your environment isn't designer-friendly. Whether it's the awful hanging ceilings and exposed fluorescent lighting, or the suits you make everyone wear to the office, or just your awful logo, your company is screaming "we have no taste". We're happy spending all day working on our ugly product in an ugly and uncomfortable place. It's not that designers are prima donnas that need funky environments, free massages, and purple walls. (Though they do love and actually need really beautiful large monitors.) It's that having great design as a foundational element of your product means having great design as a foundational element of your company's very existence. And if you don't, any decent designer can tell.

There are a couple of techniques you can use to try and entice someone good:

- Throw money at the problem. Spend big bucks and hire someone really good. This is dangerous as you don't want someone there who's only doing it for the money, but it's possibly your only first move. Especially when combined with the next point.
- Let them design everything. If you're an ugly company making

an ugly product in an ugly office, entice your potential hire with the ability not to just redesign your product, but to redesign your everything. The company. The branding. The office space. An extreme makeover. Giving this person control is more effective than giving them tons of money. Designers want to own the details. Let them. (And if you find yourself unwilling to do that, maybe you're not truly ready to have a design-led organization.)

Even if you find this person, you have to assume they won't stay forever. But creating an environment where design flourishes (with or without a senior and experienced product UX leader) is conducive to creating more of them. And that's your next strategy: If you can't find the senior UX leader you need, grow one on your own. This will take time, but it is possible. Growing your own means identifying someone who at their core is a product person, someone who lives and breathes the customer experience and has the energy, passion, and vision to deliver something customers love. This person may be inexperienced. This person may be technically green. This person may not have people leadership skills. These things can be cultivated, taught, and coached. And that's your job. Find the seed, and grow them into a towering redwood.

One tactic you can use to grow that junior person into an eventual role in leadership goes as follows. Create a virtual team of people with all the skills you need the one leader to have. You need technical expertise, business experience, marketing skills, and of course your great but junior designer. Keep this team as small as possible. Make it clear to everyone that the goal is to eventually grow the designer into the team leader. Put the most mature, socially intuitive, and non-risk-averse team member in charge of the group.

They get the final call on every decision. Even the ones not in their area of expertise. Yes this is a committee. Yes, design by committee sucks. But you have no choice. 1) By making the group small… 2) By making the term of the group finite… 3) By having the senior people realize that the junior person will eventually be in charge, and 4) by letting the junior person know that s/he has to get the trust of the senior people to eventually be in charge, you are creating a dynamic that with careful cultivation has the capability of producing 1) some great teamwork, 2) a great product design, 3) an eventual seasoned UX leader. And who knows, maybe it won't be the designer that grows into the leadership role here. Maybe you'll uncover a diamond in the rough from one of the other disciplines. Anything's possible.

Hire an outside firm. Have them do double duty designing your product, and coaching your junior design folks into more senior positions. We run our own product design firm but despite the fact that it puts us out of work eventually, we love working with great designers who work in-house at our clients. Ultimately, we find that the more confident leaders they become, the easier it is for us to do our best work. The beauty of the outside firm is they are not invested in your corporate politics. They understand the gig is limited and has pre-defined goals and metrics for success. You can even have them interview candidates for you.

This is hard stuff and requires commitment and stamina, but we promise, it's worth it.

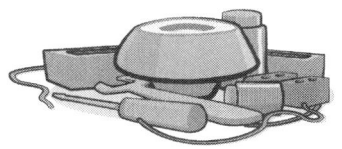

CHAPTER NINETEEN

Turning Yourself into a
User Experience Design Leader

In the last few chapters we've addressed our comments to the non-designer leadership in companies. We've advised these executives to: 1) hire great designers, 2) grow them into well-rounded design-oriented business leaders, and 3) put them in charge. But, at the end of the day, it is up to you, the designer, to grow yourself into a leader. Nobody's obliged to pave the way for you. Being a design leader is about solving problems and effective communication of your position. What better problem to solve than the one of you not being in a position to make the best product possible? In this chapter we'll give you a few suggestions on how to grow yourself into the user experience design leader you know you can be.

There are countless suggestions in books and on the Internet (and in books *on* the Internet) about how to improve yourself as designer. This list is not intended to be an exhaustive survey but rather a series of things that a) we think are the most leveraged opportunities for a young designer, and b) the things designers typically shy away from doing.

- **Present your own work.** You may (or may not) be surprised at how often good designers toil anonymously on a design team only to have someone else present, defend, and take credit for their work. If you're working on a team in a large organization, this is pretty typical. But it doesn't have to always be the case. If you make it clear to your management that you'd like to present your own work (when it's appropriate) to people outside the design team, even the most controlling manager will likely find you a way to start doing that. And the better you get, the more opportunities you'll have. Presenting your own work is not just about getting credit. Design is about communicating with the users of your proposed design. Getting your senior non-design-oriented management on board with your solutions is the first step in communicating effectively as well as you learning how to anticipate their needs and questions when you create future solutions. And, in truth, it's about credit too. Getting your name known outside your little designer enclave is important if you want to grow beyond your own discipline.

- **Get deep on design.** When you do present your own work, you'll need to defend it. It's important that you have an understanding of issues beyond design including marketing, sales, customer support, engineering and more. But the one place you get to be the authority in the room is when it comes to design and user experience. The solution? Read. Read. Read. Having a deep knowledge of history, competition, core proven concepts and best practices, and being able to articulate these facts with clarity and without defensiveness will firmly establish you as an expert in the room. When non-designers ask you to defend your work, take it as an opportunity to educate them and maybe even show off a little. If you are annoyed that they're questioning you, they'll sense your insecurity like sharks smell blood. (Sorry for the imagery, but that's how it often is.)

- **Get deeper on non-design topics as well.** It's not enough for you to be the expert on design, you need to have interest in the world around you – specifically the world of your company's business. You may not be the expert on the engineering or sales of your product but that doesn't mean you shouldn't know about new technologies that may be of benefit to your product, or of competition's sales tactics. A great way to get up-to-speed on other areas is to talk routinely to friends and mentors from other areas of the organization. Most people are excited to share their expertise. This is also another key way for you to make yourself known outside of the design team.

- **Opine on non-design issues.** Once you actually get to present your own work outside of the design team, it's great for you to be the expert on design in the room, but that's not enough. Just because you're not an expert in other areas, doesn't mean you can't have thoughtful opinions on other matters. You've been reading. You have mentors. You have ideas. Share them. A designer's creativity is not bound to Photoshop. Designers are problem solvers. And please, whatever you do, please don't preface every non-design comment with "Well, from a design perspective…". Your opinion is from your perspective. And your perspective is the product of your experience in design and a whole variety of other interests and knowledge you've been carefully cultivating. If you feel strongly about something, and can articulate your thoughts clearly, speak up.

Remember, you can be an ally to non-design colleagues when they are defending their work. Having solid cross-discipline relationships can only help as you try to make your designs come to fruition across the broader organization.

You may notice a theme running throughout most of our recommendations — getting out of your comfort zone. Not all designers are introverts, but it's understandable why those that are more comfortable communicating visually, might tend to avoid situations where they need to get in front of a group and defend their ideas. Being a designer is not just about creating solutions, it's about getting the broader team on board with those solutions in order to take your design to market. And they can't get behind you if they don't even know who you are.

CHAPTER TWENTY

Destroying Your Enemies
Through the Magic of Design

Hierarchical organizations large and small are rife with politics. In fact, the smaller the stakes, the more vicious they can be. Political organizations are ones where what things look like are just as, or more, important as what you actually do. Dealing with perceptions as well as ego and insecurity is part of dealing with human beings. This is who we are. And as soon as we create situations where there are winners and losers we create politics. And fighting. In some organizations, regardless of how brilliant your design may be, the politics will kill your plans before they have a chance to really blossom. And that's a shame.

The single most important thing you can understand about navigating the gauntlet of organizational politics is the relative risks of saying no vs. yes. Your job, your dream, your passion is to say "yes". Yes to your product vision. Yes to your design. Yes to delighting customers. But the road is littered with opponents. These are people who will raise concerns about your proposals, reasonable sounding concerns. Concerns that may or may not be genuine. Maybe they're good thoughts to consider that have been offered in good faith, and maybe they're just obstacles designed to trip you up and damage you as a competitor in the organization. If you suspect an opponent's motivations are personal, you'll never prove it. That only happens in the movies. In effect, their motivations are irrelevant. Genuine or jerky, your only remaining option is to deal with their issues at face value.

But how?

Before we answer, let's pause for an anecdote.

Years ago we worked on one of two teams in the same company that worked on competing projects. This happens often. The company's leadership hopes competition fosters innovation, and people bringing forth their best ideas. The other team was huge and had been working on their project for years. There were smart and talented people on that team doing good work. They even had good design talent, but the team wasn't design driven. They were technology driven. This is not to say that they didn't think about customers. They did. It's just that the high order bit was their technology choice, and then they did their best to design around those choices.

Our team was small. We had decent ideas and were design led. Our team fashioned a high-fidelity prototype that illustrated our ideas. It was on rails, a glorified slide show. And it was gorgeous. The other team had code. We had beautiful images that moved.

As things came to a head politically, we finally revealed our design to the other team. After the presentation, they looked like they'd been punched in the stomach. Even though they had code, we just had a better story. We had something inspiring. Their stuff was flat. And boring. Literally and metaphorically. And even though they were creative and smart, the genetics of their team had led them down an uninspiring path. They knew it. And so did the execs who saw both teams' work.

Within a week those execs tried to merge our teams. And when it was clear that we were culturally incompatible, their project was killed. Was our design work solely responsible for the end of their project? No. Was it one of the things that sent them over the edge? Without a doubt.

Now let's return to our discussion of how you can deal with the people who oppose your plans in your organization. Your first choice is to use the logic of your arguments, your personal charm, and maybe a little horse-trading to get those folks on board. And in many cases that works. It's always your best option. We're big fans of working together harmoniously. But the larger the organization (and it doesn't have to be all that large) the higher the odds that there will be some people where reasoned discussion and collaboration doesn't work. Ever.

Remember, the political economics of saying "no" in large organizations are so much better than saying "yes". Saying "no" costs essentially nothing. You don't need to prove anything. You'll almost never be proven wrong for saying no. And the optics are great too. The person saying "yes" looks overly enthusiastic, while the person saying "no" in reasonable tones sounds like the grownup. The naysayer just has to raise reasonable doubt to save the company from wasting time and money on some "foolish and poorly thought out initiative". However, saying "yes" is costly. You're putting yourself out on a limb. You're being specific. You're opening yourself up to attack. You're trying to do something.

As a user experience design leader you have a secret advantage. It's the thing that often overcomes every opponent, every craven naysayer. It's the High Fidelity Visualization.

What is the High Fidelity Visualization? It could be anything from a series of beautiful UI mockups, to a user experience prototype on rails, to a freeform prototype that the audience can try themselves, to a beautifully produced video showing customers using the prototype.

There will always be "no" people. But "no" people rarely have counter-proposals. And when they do, they're usually vague or a set of yawn-inducing PowerPoint bullets. By definition, they don't want to be out on a limb or they'd be subject to attack. So they keep things light on details. But when you show up with a High Fidelity Visualization, if you've done your job, and told a great story, everyone else in the room will fall in love with your plan. Decision makers will get excited. They'll start defending your ideas against the naysayers. Emotion motivates them to become advocates for your plan, your story. And this is a good thing.

But take note, we liken these visualizations to nuclear weapons. They're incredibly powerful tools and can cause collateral damage. You've got to get the dosage just right. Sometimes you can do such a good job getting your company's leadership on board with your ideas that now they bother you every week to find out why the product isn't done yet. After all, that prototype looked essentially ready to ship, and you didn't spend a lot of time in your pitch meeting talking about the smoke and mirrors you used to put it together.

The point is this: with a beautifully executed High Fidelity Visualization that sets the right tone, you can neutralize the people in your organization who love to say "no". This is your secret advantage as someone with vision, an ability to visualize your plan and bring it to life in people's imagination, and the leadership skills to deliver on that vision. Tell the right story with your execution here and anyone who's getting in your way will fall by the wayside.

And for those of you who feel this is militaristic in tone, you're right. Hierarchical organizations with more than ten people on the team invariably have a representative population of personality types — including people who will get in your way. If you really want to make something special and deliver it to customers, then you need to get the doubters on board or run them over. Partnering with the doubters is always preferable as long as it's not at the expense of your ideas. But unfortunately, it's not always possible. It's not personal. It's not about being a jerk. It's not about beating your chest. It's about making something great. And if you're in an organization where people with limited vision and possibly political aims are forever stopping you from delivering something wonderful, you need to arm yourself and fight. Spending your time arguing endlessly with people so you can deliver a watered-down version of the great thing that resides in your head is a waste of your time.

How do you know which feedback is killing your vision and which is making it better? Listen to everyone, open your mind, but trust your instincts. If you stick to your guns and fail, at least you'll learn something. If you turn your ideas into some sort of compromise mish-mash and you fail, you'll never know exactly what caused the failure and you truly will have wasted your time.

Good luck soldier.

Artefact

Vanessa Fox

Greg Storey

Christian Hagel

Scott Berkun

Natala Menezes

Peyman Oreizy

Deborah Dubrow

David D'Souza

Ray Palermo

Rachel Lanham

Sarah Bird

Sylvain Galineau

Alice Merchant

Stephen Dossick

Chris Evans

Marc Hedlund

Joseph Dickerson

Arlys Osborne

Amanda Powter

Jennifer Winters

paul jennings

Amir Koren

Deborah Hamel

Kevin Wong

Tom Berry

Ryan Schroeder

Adrian Klein

Adam Kinney

Si Daniels

Adam Phillabaum

Vinny Pasceri

Greg Pascale

Debra Weissman

Jerry Koh

Josh Santangelo

Kyle Kesterson

John

Evonne Benedict

Jennifer Sukis

Tom Kirby-Green

Azmir Saliefendic

Tom Tokarski

Michelle Goldberg

Kirill Zubovsky

Christen Coomer

inkblot

Matt Haughey

Bill Bliss

Anna Bevens

Marcelo Calbucci

Wendy Wolk Ryan

Kushal Chakrabarti

Paige Pauli

Tonya Engst

Narisa

Michele Freed

Brittany Staten

Ernest Lansford

Henry Rose

Eric Theriault

Keller Smith

Joel Stimson
Larry
Will Miceli
Ed Allard
Alex Hopmann
Greg Hochmuth
Jeff Ort
Linda Paton
Rich Schoenrock
Muness Castle
Ravi Chandrasekaran
Mark Bottomley
Rachel
Eric Nehrlich
Matt
Nate Miller
Paul Anguiano
Megan
Rebecca Lovell
Nishant Kothary
Mamie Rheingold
James Collins
Adam Doppelt
Rachel Doppelt
Aarron Walter
Doug Hanke
Nadja Haldimann
Michael Hart Leggett
Steven Glickman
Danielle Sheffler
Sarah Mackinnon

Chris Carter
Nick Grace
Matt Grommes
Kav Latiolais
Yoni Shechter
Jeremy Wemple
Jeff Whitmire
Amy Gorrek
David Sutoyo
Jan Molendijk
Dwight Battle
Tyesha
Ward Meremans
Jeff Boyus
Brittany
Bootstrapper Studios
Erwin Werkman
Kevin Lucca
Jonny McConnell
Cathie Toshach
Donovan
Josh Peters
Tommy Lewis
Dan Vogel
kaleemux
Cyriel van 't End
Brad Serbus
Andrew
Jamie Cabaccang
Kevin Davis

ACKNOWLEDGMENTS

Surprisingly, this may be the most daunting section of this book to write. Our names are biggest on the cover, but this book was the creation of many more people than just us. Our amazingly patient Kickstarter supporters were so numerous we've given them their own thank you section. But that doesn't cover everyone.

Scott Berkun is a colleague and a friend who we've known and worked with for over a decade. Scott has shown us all the model for taking your expertise and sharing it generously and thoughtfully with the industry and the world. His feedback both broad and specific on this undertaking has been invaluable. We're thrilled to have him as the editor of this book.

Tom Chang is a colleague at Jackson Fish Market who's presence really pushed the book forward and over the finish line. We'd written the text awhile ago. And while we had more work to do on the content, we ran into some dead ends in terms of illustration. Tom brought his steady hands and creative mind to the book and gave us a fresh look and feel as well as illustrations that truly illuminate many of the points we were trying to make. The book wouldn't have been the same without his incredible art.

Holly Dunning, McKenna Phillabaum, and Candy Chan make up the rest of our Jackson Fish colleagues. They contributed in countless ways large and small. Most often giving us the time and leeway to focus on delivering the book with quality to a waiting (and patient) audience. We're so grateful that we get to work with them every day.

Fantastic copyediting was provided by Debra Weissman who always gives selflessly to our efforts and to whom we'll be eternally grateful. Additional copyediting was generously sent by our Kickstarter supporters, especially Eric Lawrence who went through the text with a fine tooth comb.

Our industry colleagues have inspired us over the years to do our best. Rather than be competitive, they've shown us nothing but support and encouragement for creating our small firm and the work we do there. Jackson Fish Market is still a relatively small concern, but it's grown into something solid and real and special in no small part because of the friendships we've made in the design and tech fields.

And most importantly, we'd like to thank our clients. Jackson Fish Market is first and foremost a holistic user experience design consultancy. Dozens of clients over the years have put their faith and trust in us to shepherd their brands and their software experiences to customers in a way that represents their genuine passions and concerns. We take this responsibility seriously. Not only has the work they've given us helped us build our business, but it has given us the collective insight and (hopefully) wisdom that we've shared in the pages of this book. Little did they know it, but as often as we were teaching them about design and user experience, they were teaching us just as much.

Finally, we'd like to thank our family and friends who cheer us on with every new project, initiative, and creation. We're so grateful their unflagging support.

Thanks to everyone. We hope this book can in some small way give back to all those that have helped us to get to this point.

Hillel & Jenny

16581684R00069

Made in the USA
San Bernardino, CA
10 November 2014